BE DO GIVE LOVE

BE DO GIVE LOVE

YOUR LIFE STORY IN FOUR WORDS

ERIK LARSON

WITH
MADAILEIN LARSON

CoROIN BOOKS

Published by Coroin Books
coroin.com/books

Cover and illustrations commissioned by Coroin Books
Artwork by **Carlos Maraver**
vectorlance.com

eBook ISBN: 978-1-963770-00-1
Paperback ISBN: 978-1-963770-01-8
Hardcover ISBN: 978-1-963770-02-5

LCCN (Library of Congress Control Number): 2025944144

The authors and publisher have made every effort to ensure that the information in this book is accurate at the time of publication. Neither the authors nor the publisher shall be held liable for any loss, damage, or disruption caused by errors or omissions, whether such errors result from negligence, accident, or any other cause. Readers are encouraged to verify any information before taking action.

Dedicated to
the Author & Pilot,
the Captain,
the Fighting Lady,
the Princess,
and Love Immortal

Love covers the past.
Love comforts the present.
Love continues into the future.

CONTENTS

HOWDY!

Time slows down for a handful of events in life.

Death is one of them.

We ask questions during crisis and find clarity later.

This book is the story of the year where everything fell apart.

And had to be put back together.

It was a year of much reflection and writing.

Of countless conversations with friends and family. I talked with colleagues and business partners, and anyone who would listen.

The whirlwind of insanity going around in my head was a jumbled mess of unresolved questions that led to more questions.

I'm forever grateful for the conversations with my daughter, Maddie, as we traveled together on planes, trains, and automobiles to attend events that spring and summer.

Her probing and unpacking, pushing for meaning and clarity, helped me untangle the knots and really connect the dots.

This book would be incomplete and rather boring if it were only my voice coming from the pages.

The chapters that follow are primarily me (Erik) sharing a few stories from my past that connect to these Four Words, complete with my 50-year-old perspective and some lessons learned.

At the end of each chapter are insights and questions to ponder from Maddie and her 20-year-old perspective.

Erik and Maddie in New Orleans, April 2025

At some point that summer, we realized we had something in common, besides having the same last name.

Even though we are obviously from different generations, the big questions in life that we were both asking (the ones that keep us up at night) were surprisingly the same:

Who am I (really)?

What am I doing with my life?

What difference does it make?

Why does any of this matter?

For anyone who has managed to function well for a long time and recognizes that management isn't the problem, productivity isn't the missing ingredient, and more controls aren't the answer, this book is for you!

Please no more quick-fixes and tips, tricks, and techniques!

You won't find that stuff in here.

The stories are real.

The reflections are raw.

May you find hope, encouragement, and most of all LOVE.

THE FOUR WORDS

For a long time, I thought I had it figured out.

Not life exactly, but certainly how to move through it. How to make stuff happen and keep it all together.

How to more than just get by.

I'm not saying I created some ground-breaking system or brilliant framework. It's more like I discovered something of great value, a lost treasure chest containing timeless truth.

It started with three simple verbs: BE, DO, and HAVE.

The order was important. The words are a progression:

BE → DO → HAVE

In my head, the Three Words were beautifully connected:

Know who you are (BE), your identity, passions, purpose

Focus your efforts and actions (DO) into making

Dreams become reality (HAVE)

Simple, right?

Clear. Concise. Logical. Linear.

Underneath the fun wordplay and creative metaphors in every program and practice I saw were those same Three Words:

BE → DO → HAVE

As I was sharing this with Maddie, I drew a few "napkin sketches" to help show and tell. Here's the first one:

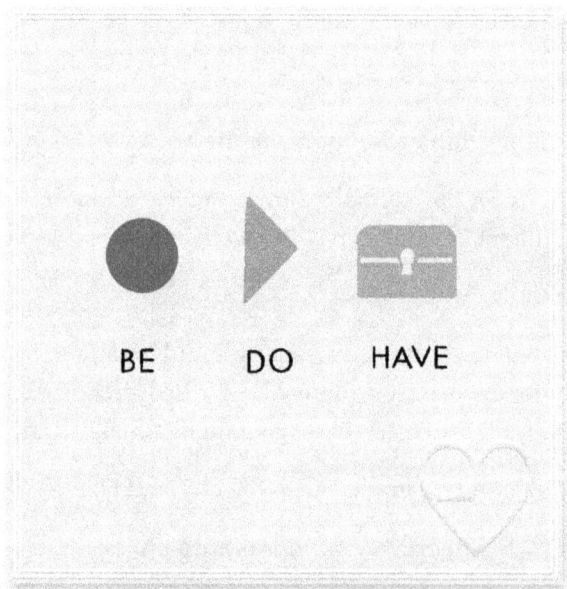

Napkin Sketch BE DO HAVE

Hard work and discipline are the keys to success.

Success is measured by accumulation.

Yup, the formula checks out.

Until it doesn't.

Until you wake up one day and realize you're exhausted and surrounded by noise with a to-do list a mile long that you couldn't care less about.

And you wonder what the heck any of it means and why any of it matters anyway. Something was missing.

What about generosity and helping people?

What about legacy and impact?

There was a fourth word.

Another verb.

GIVE.

There is no separating BE and DO. The real question on GIVE was: did it go before or after HAVE?

Option A - tack GIVE on to the end:

BE → DO → HAVE → GIVE

Generosity flows out of abundance.

That tracks with stories of early 20th century philanthropists:

BE really awesome at what you DO and then you will HAVE so much that it's only natural to GIVE some away and setup foundations and endowments for the benefit of others.

Good stuff, I thought. Logical. Who can GIVE something they don't first HAVE?

On the other hand …

Option B - put GIVE in the middle:

BE → DO → GIVE → HAVE

Generosity is a part of abundance.

The wealthy people I know have a track record of generosity that started in their early days, before the fame and fortune.

That was pretty compelling, because they're not just characters in a book, but real people I have spent time with across the years and in some cases decades.

A spirited debate went on in my mind and on whiteboards.

Does **Option A** make more sense

HAVE → GIVE

Or was it **Option B**

GIVE → HAVE

In the end, Option B won out. Mainly because I could not separate it from the first two words, BE and DO.

GIVE is not an afterthought or an add-on.

It's the natural extension of our Identity to Actions to Impact:

BE → DO → GIVE

When actions (DO) are connected to passions (BE) the result is an unforced, outward-flowing, positive impact (GIVE).

Unforced.

Natural.

The Words resonated more as a quartet. It was at this point that I really thought I had something.

And so for many years, it was settled.

The Four Words, in proper sequence, were:

BE → DO → GIVE → HAVE

Here's the updated napkin sketch:

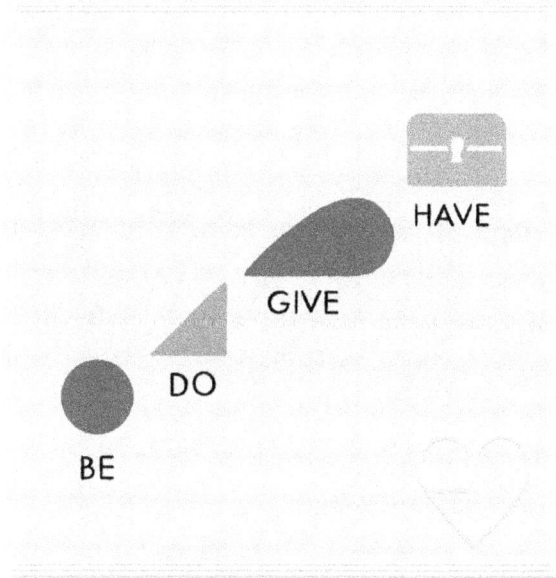

Napkin Sketch BE DO GIVE HAVE

That was fine, until the year where everything changed.

THE FIRST TWO WORDS

JELLYFISH!

SUMMER ~1980: CORPUS CHRISTI

I t was 1980-something, Corpus Christi, Texas, condo on the beach. We had driven down from Dallas for what was destined to be the most incredible vacation ever.

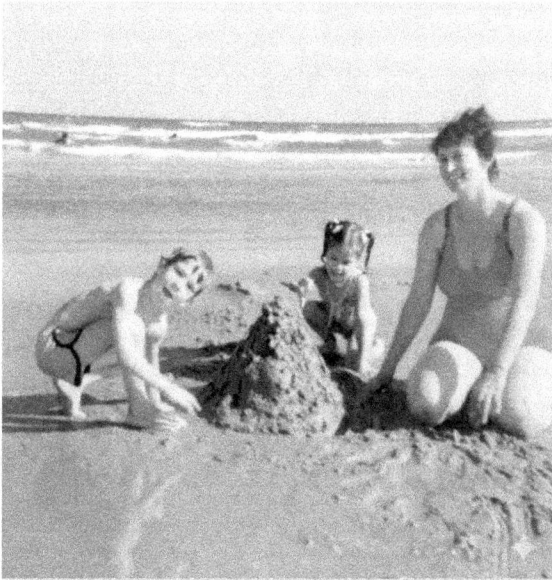

Erik, Julie, and Mom in Corpus Christi, 1980s

I love the ocean. My sister was too young to go in the water, so she and my dad played in the sand.

My mom and I were in the waves, trying to body surf. I wasn't very good at it, as I recall. We were splashing about and having a great time trying not to drink half of the Gulf.

And then I remember something strange.

A warm sensation, first on my leg.

Then it was my arm.

Then my back.

Before long, my entire body was on fire.

I looked over at my mom. I was starting to freak out.

She was calm, grabbed my hand, and we raced out of the water, across the sand, up the stairs, and into the cold air conditioning inside the condo.

My mom disappeared into the kitchen and started rummaging through the pantry and cabinets, looking for something. I had no idea what.

Meanwhile, I was laying on an itchy couch, moaning and flailing about, convinced my skin was melting off.

The next part is a little fuzzy in my memory.

Did my mom find what she was looking for right away or had I passed out on the couch while she ran to the store, regaining consciousness right when she returned? I can't recall.

The next thing I remember was the cure that made the pain stop.

It was Meat Tenderizer!

A nasty smelling combination of salt and spices did the trick that day and somehow put out the fire so my skin could cool.

Later that evening, our family took a walk on the beach around sunset. There were hundreds of jellyfish washed up on the shore, semi-transparent blobs dotting the beach for as far as we could see.

I wanted to pick one up and fling it like a frisbee, but my mom stopped me. Even though the tentacles were gone, she pointed out, the jellyfish caps also contain the *nematocysts* — the microscopic venom-guns that fire on contact.

You could still get stung!

Those guns were still locked and loaded.

An autonomous, distributed weapons system.

Armed and dangerous, even after death. Incredible!

———

When I think about the first word, BE, two things come to mind:

1. My mom
2. Jellyfish

My mom believed that everyone is one-of-a-kind.

You are unique. You have a unique calling, something specific that only you can bring into this world.

She encouraged us to be ourselves.

> Be true to yourself.

> Recognize how you are different.

> Have courage and lean into that uniqueness.

> Appreciate your one-of-a-kind design. It's a gift. Use it.

And then jellyfish.

These fascinating creatures have some very specialized features, more than just the autonomous defense system.

For example, their bell shape design allows them to move through the water like a rocket. This is nearly effortless, making them the most energy efficient swimmers in the ocean.

But they don't always move like that. Most of the time, they just drift around with the current.

Under the black lights at Moody Gardens Aquarium, in what looks like a room full of giant lava lamps, Hazel (my granddaughter) and I love to watch the jellyfish float around in their tall cylindrical tanks.

Erik and Hazel at Moody Gardens Aquarium, March 2025

There are so many different species on display.

Each tank has tens or hundreds of jellyfish of the same species. And as you look closer, every single one is slightly different.

Unique. Individual. Specialized.

We're all a little bit like jellyfish.

Sometimes wandering aimlessly, forgetting that we have a unique, specialized design. Our super-power.

But when we do lean into that super-power, that's when we become unstoppable.

One vast ocean. Infinite possibilities.

Maddie's Perspective

Knowing who you are is not as easy as it sounds. Parents, teachers, and friends (usually with good intentions) tell you who they think you are.

Who they think you should be.

Who they want you to be.

And if their words resonate, feel free to use them to help you go through this process of self-identification.

But if they don't, it's fine. Allow those words to float on by.

Take time to figure out who you are, because it matters.

Questions to Ponder:

1. What are some words that describe you? (Only include positive words. This is not a list of shortcomings).

2. What experiences bring joy to your life? What activities make you feel alive?

3. What are some of your favorite memories? And why?

4. What do you want to be known for?

A GENTLE PUSH

SPRING BREAK 1984: NEW MEXICO

I n our family, this story has been told more times and been
embellished more than all the others combined.

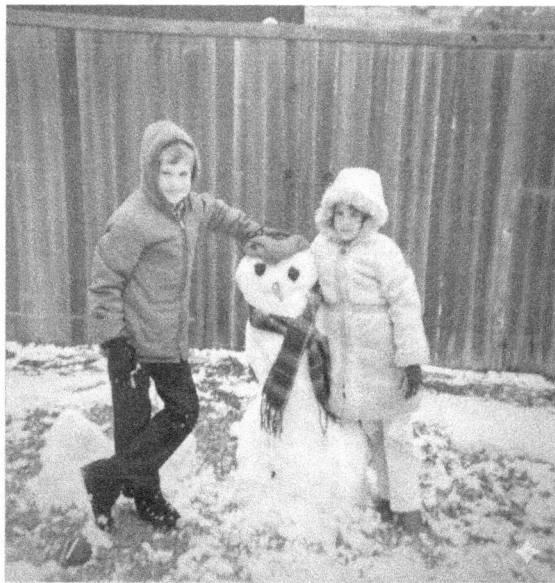

Erik and Julie enjoying snow in Dallas, 1980s

Growing up in Dallas, we rarely had snow (and not a lot of it).

Every couple years, we'd get one or two, maybe three inches of snow if we were really lucky. Hopefully there would be enough to build a lopsided snowman.

Winter precipitation was usually the rock-hard kind: ice, not snow. North Texas is also mostly flat and therefore not conducive to fun winter activities like they have in the mountains.

Or so we heard. My sister and I were still waiting to experience a real winter vacation.

This year that would all change. We were going skiing!

Heading west out of Denver towards the mountains and ski resorts, I noticed there was already snow on the ground.

And snow was still coming down, gently floating through the air until it landed on a tree or a roof or the ground.

There was snow everywhere.

My sister and I couldn't wait to get to the lodge and have a snowball fight or build a snowman.

As we started making our way up the mountain, I noticed the car slipping and sliding a little.

My mom was concerned.

My sister and I thought it was fun.

Safety prevailed.

My dad pulled over to put the chains on the tires. The roads were starting to freeze over, and it was getting dark.

A truck driver who knew that road well told him that our rear-wheel drive car (even with chains) would not safely make it up the pass in these conditions.

We should turn around.

What? No!

There was snow all around us, and now we can't even get to the place where we could actually play in the snow.

Too much of a good thing was now a bad thing.

We turned around and headed back to Denver for the night. Barring some kind of weather miracle, our grand plans for a fantastic ski vacation in the mountains were about to disintegrate.

The next day, the car wouldn't start. My dad and I walked to get a can of starter fluid to pour into the carburetor.

It started. Amazing!

Unfortunately, there was no weather miracle. The road conditions had worsened overnight. So we packed up the car and headed south.

———

On the way back to Texas, somewhere in New Mexico, my dad spotted an opportunity.

A tiny piece of winter redemption. A state park that wasn't exactly open but also technically wasn't closed.

Translation:

> The state park was open enough for us to "stretch our legs."

And stretch our legs, we did.

Once the car stopped, my sister and I jumped out and raced toward the tallest hill we could find.

Let the fun begin.

We ran up and down the hill, leaping into a deep pile of powdery snow and crawling out.

Over and over and over again.

One time at the top of the hill, we called down to my mom to climb up and join in the fun. With more than a little hesitation, she started to make her way up to the top.

I like to think of this scene as one of those wholesome, picture-perfect, Norman Rockwell family moments ready to be captured and immortalized.

My dad went back to the car to get his camera.

My sister demonstrated the proper technique:

> Run as fast as possible
> down the hill and launch
> into a nice fluffy snowbank.

Easy peasy.

At the bottom, my sister popped up with arms raised like an Olympic gymnast who nailed the dismount.

She motioned for my mom to come down and join her.

My mom froze.

We exchanged words. I don't remember the specifics, but I had this feeling she needed some encouragement.

And that encouragement came in the form of a little nudge.

Just to be clear: It was not a shove.

It was a gentle push.

And apparently that was enough, because gravity took over.

My mom started flying down the hill*.

My dad would later say he'd never seen her run so fast.

She had accelerated far beyond the recommended speed limit for moms on snowy hillsides.

When she got to the bottom of the hill, she ran straight towards my sister. Actually, she ran right *over* my sister, and they both disappeared into the snow.

A two-person snowball.

I didn't hesitate.

No thinking needed.

I did what any elementary-school boy would do.

I raced down the hill as fast as I could, soared through the air with arms out like airplane wings, and expertly navigated the landing.

Right on top of the dogpile.

When I rolled off and looked up, a single tiny snowflake drifted down and landed on my nose.

It was a magical moment.

I had completely forgotten about the long boring car ride, the treacherous mountain pass, the disappointment of not being able to ski. All I was thinking about was how much fun I was having right now. I couldn't wait to go again.

I sat up, grinning, and looked over at my mom and sister.

They were slowly getting up.

_____

* It was just a hill. However, it is commonly, but mistakenly, referred to as a "mountain" when this story is told at family gatherings (i.e., "Did you really push your mom down the mountain?").

And for a moment, everything was silent.

Then came the line that has echoed through my childhood:

> *Erik Richard Larson, that is the most asinine thing you have ever done in your entire life.*

At the time, I didn't know what "asinine" meant.

I wondered if it was somewhere between an *ass-8* and an *ass-10*. Context clues led me to believe that whatever the meaning, it was not good.

And that was the end of our fun snow adventure.

It's also where the telling of this story usually ends. If you were wondering what happened next, we got back in the car and drove (silently) for hours and hours. We stopped at a forgettable motel somewhere in west Texas that night before finally getting back home the next day.

My dad recently reminded me that my mom had a headache for two days, which would be the whole way back and then some.

My sister was fine, just in case you were wondering.

What amazes me now, as I reflect back 40+ years later, isn't what my mom said. Words matter.

It's what she did *not* say that sticks with me.

She didn't say *I was* asinine, or that *I was* an ass (or any of the other colorful variations of that word).

She said that *what I did* was asinine.

My actions (DO) and my identity (BE) were not to be confused.

She corrected the action, she didn't attack my identity.

She was focused first on who I was (BE) and pointed out the obvious disconnect with what I did (DO).

The distinction between being and doing has become clearer with time. What you do does not define who you are.

We all make mistakes. Bad choices don't erase your worth.

My mom never weaponized this story against me or turned it into a badge of shame. Quite the opposite, really.

She laughed whenever it was told, and sometimes laughed so hard she cried. She made it a family legend, not a family wound.

The foundation of the first two words, BE and DO, was always there. We look first to identify and then to behavior.

BE → DO

Maddie's Perspective

This story was told at so many family gatherings I remember. Gramma laughed and laughed. We all did.

My dad's youthful behavior lacked good judgment and maturity, for sure.

But it really wasn't that much out of character for him.

In other words, maybe his identity (BE) was in alignment with his actions (DO). As a child, he was adventurous and encouraging.

He wanted to have fun and wanted everyone, including his mom, to have fun.

That doesn't mean his actions were acceptable.

> Please don't push moms (or anyone else) down mountains!

The mistake was when he assumed his mom was equally adventurous. She was adventurous, but not like that.

The point here is that it doesn't really work when we project our identity and the things we are passionate about (BE) onto someone else. It's understandable why they won't be as excited and eager as we are.

Questions to Ponder:

1. How aligned are your actions with your identity? Do your actions reflect who you are?

2. Can you give yourself some grace for a past mistake? Recognize that many mistakes are a behavior that is out of alignment with our identity.

3. When other people make mistakes, especially when it affects you, what would help you remember to correct the behavior without attacking the person?

VEGAS, BABY!
MAY 2025: MGM GRAND

Maddie

I'd been to Vegas before, but never like this. There were two hotel suites filled with twenty high-level speakers, consultants, and coaches.

People who live on stages. People who joke about microphones being like ice cream cones.

These are people my dad calls "the real pros."

Walking in felt like stumbling into the grown-ups' table at Thanksgiving, except the grown-ups here had bestselling books, keynote reels, and frequent flyer status that bordered on supernatural.

Meanwhile, I was the only Gen Zer in the room.

My assignment?

To co-lead a session on generational communication.

Translation: *represent my entire age group while a room full of professionals tries to solve me like a puzzle.*

No pressure.

This trip was part of my internship, but that word makes it sound more official than it felt.

Since March, I'd been helping my dad get Boo's books ready for the world. Boo is the name everyone called my great-grandfather.

I never met him. I was born the year after he died, but I had heard lots of stories about him.

Our job in 2025 was to get the books in print and even into the Library of Congress (which Gramma, my grandmother, the librarian would especially appreciate).

I started editing on a road trip in March and was still editing when we went to New Orleans in April. Now it was Memorial Day week, and we were in Vegas.

My dad looked relaxed, maybe too relaxed.

Arms crossed, a casual little smile, like he'd just wandered in from the casino after a winning streak. Meanwhile, my stomach was twisting itself into balloon animals.

The session started with snacks and small talk, but within minutes the tone shifted.

Someone asked what the afternoon session was actually about.

"Understanding how to connect across generations," someone said.

"And lucky for us, we have a real Gen Zer in the room."

Twenty heads swiveled toward me.

Fantastic, I thought.

The questions came rapid-fire:

- Does the label Gen Z mean anything to you?
- What are we getting wrong about your generation?
- Are attention spans shorter?
- How do we market to you?
- What platform do you trust?

It didn't feel like a conversation.

It was starting to feel like a strategy meeting with me as the case study.

They weren't talking to me.

They were trying to decode me.

And then someone asked, "So what would make you hire a speaker?"

I tried. I really did.

"I... don't know? Your question is too..."

I shrugged.

There were too many voices, too many angles, too much all at once. I couldn't even find the starting line.

"I don't know what you're asking. Why would I hire a speaker?"

The room paused. Then laughter.

Whew.

"That's helpful," someone said.

"We need to rethink how we ask questions," said another.

"No, really. This is gold," said a third.

I blinked.

I had done absolutely nothing except tell the truth.

They leaned in.

They were actually listening.

They weren't hunting for tactics anymore.

Someone asked about misconceptions older generations have about Gen Z.

> I'm not always on my phone.
>
> I actually hate virtual.
>
> Staring at a screen without
>
> being able to feel the room
>
> just drains me.
>
> I'd rather be in person.
>
> This world is full of noise.
>
> There's too much input.
>
> With too many rules.
>
> It is way too easy
>
> to screw up.

Pens hit notepads.

Another asked about online permanence.

So I told them the real stuff.

> I untagged every photo where I had a drink in my hand before sorority recruitment.
>
> I privatized my TikTok because I am scared a future employer or client will judge me.

I deleted a skydiving picture because I was using 'inappropriate' sign language.

Maddie Skydiving, April 2023

A nice cybersecurity guy raised his hand and said, "That has big implications not just for my clients but for me, personally."

"I have kids," he continued. "And I've never thought about it from that perspective."

Heads around the room were nodding.

This is not the conversation I thought we'd be having.

Then came questions about attention, trust, and content.

"Tie this together for us," someone asked. "How do we reach your generation?"

"For us?" I said.

TikTok is our Google.

I kept going.

> If something's interesting, I'll go deeper.
>
> Short form leads to long form.
>
> But if you can't hook me in fifteen seconds, you lost me.
>
> It's about earning the right to get me to go deeper.
>
> And please, just because my attention span is short, doesn't mean you should rush your thoughts.
>
> Your thoughts outrun your words, and I can't follow you.

Half the room started writing like their careers depended on it.

> Don't lead with your book or whatever you're selling.
>
> Say what you want people to know first.
>
> Get straight to the point.
>
> No fluff.

Oh no. I hope I didn't just offend half the people in the room.

They were still taking notes.

"So clarity before credentials?" someone asked.

"Just don't overcomplicate the message," I said.

"And calm down on all the cringy AI backgrounds."

More scribbling.

"What keeps you up at night?" someone asked.

"Stress," I said. "Admissions officers."

Laughter.

But then I added something that wasn't funny.

> It's not FOMO: fear of missing out.

> It's FOFU: fear of "messing" up.

> Fear of being wrong.

> There are so many ways to fail.

> And everyone has an opinion about the "right" way you should (or shouldn't) do absolutely every thing.

The room went still.

I was giving them truth, not platitudes.

These were professionals with stage-presence superpowers. Their fear just had fancier packaging.

After the session, I had some really nice thank yous, each in their own way.

> "You helped me understand my daughter."
> "I need to rethink my content."
> "You're incredibly authentic."

I didn't come to Vegas planning on teaching anyone anything. I was looking forward to a fun working vacation.

I thought I would be attending meetings, not presenting. Then I got all nervous and convinced myself I didn't belong.

But somewhere between *I don't know what you're asking* and *TikTok is our Google*, I stopped worrying about my performance and just told them the raw truth.

Erik and Maddie in Las Vegas, May 2025

They told me that my honesty changed how they thought about their work, their kids, and their questions.

Apparently, the truth was what they wanted.

I was just being myself.

It reminded me:

Everyone has something to contribute to the conversation.

Questions to Ponder:

1. In what situations do you feel pressured to perform instead of being yourself?

2. Who are you when you stop performing, when you're not trying to prove you belong or to fit in?

3. Think of a relationship in your life that might benefit from more authenticity. What is getting in the way of trust and a deeper connection?

HAVE IS THE PROBLEM

SCARCITY SUCKS
EARLY 1980S: MCDONALD'S

S carcity is one of the most damaging concepts that we've normalized and baked into our society. You can hear it in our everyday speech:

Money doesn't grow on trees
We're stretched too thin
We can't afford that
Don't have time
Zero-sum

For as long as I can remember, the principle of scarcity has been a core part of my belief system.

Resources are limited and time is finite.

Common sense.

It's right there in the wisdom of saving for a rainy day.

It's even disguised and celebrated as a virtue: frugality.

Scarcity is the big bad wolf dressed up in the sheep's clothing.

Growing up in an affluent suburban community in the 1980s, I never thought we were poor.

I also knew we weren't rich.

Driving home after a soccer game, we stopped at McDonald's for a treat. Back then, a soft-serve cone cost ten cents.

Ten cents.

So that means for less than a dollar, our whole family could have a sweet treat.

As we pulled into the drive thru, my dad said, "Four cones" almost like it was a question.

My mom smiled and said, "Yes, please!"

I nodded.

My sister asked, "Can I get a Happy Meal?"

I couldn't believe it.

A Happy Meal cost $1.50.

Didn't she know that "money doesn't grow on trees"?

I waited for the rebuke. It never came.

My dad drove up to the clown-faced speaker box, rolled down his window and said, "Three cones and a Happy Meal with a Coke, please."

After a long pause, the speaker crackled, and a voice said, "That will be $1.89. Please drive around."

Pretty soon, I smelled fresh french fries in the seat beside me.

My ice-cream cone didn't taste good anymore.

It's not like I wanted the fries. I wanted ice cream. I wanted everyone to have the same thing. Made sense to me.

The funny thing is that of the four people in that car, I am the only one who remembers this story. It wasn't meaningful to my mom, dad, or sister.

Can you believe it?

For years, I held myself up as some kind of unsung hero in the story. It was a good example of how I appreciated and honored the thrift and sacrifice of my parents. I was doing my part to make sure we had enough and didn't run out.

Didn't run out!

Did you catch that? That's scarcity right there.

It's the encoding of HAVE into my mindset.

Scarcity is fear.

Fear that you'll run out.

Fear there won't be enough to go around.

Or maybe just not enough for you.

Fear is a helluva motivator.

It starts us down the road to justifying those long hours, the time away from family, the mental anguish, and whatever else we tell ourselves we have to do to "put food on the table," so to speak.

Few people in this world are immune from scarcity.

Seems like it's baked into the human experience.

The other day, my five year old granddaughter was painting.

She was working on a picture of a bird and needed to add some blue paint for the background.

Watching her squeeze acrylic paint out of the tube and onto the palette, I found myself thinking:

Woah! Careful there. Don't squeeze too much.

I didn't say it out loud. It was just a gigantic thought-balloon coming out of my head. Full of fear.

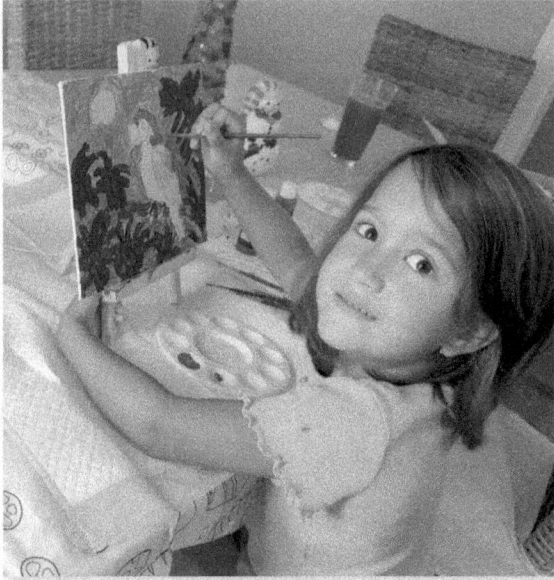

Hazel Painting Birds, December 2025

A few minutes later, she needed a new color.

This time it was adding white to lighten up red and make a nice rose hue for the flower petals.

She picked up the white and started to squeeze some on top of the red. I couldn't stop myself.

I made an "observation" that we were running low on white.

Oops.

Thankfully it didn't phase her.

Maybe she is immune to the sickness of scarcity?

I hope it doesn't get a grip on her someday the way it has me. If scarcity was a splinter, I would say, *it's in there pretty deep.*

Five minutes later, I was placing an order online to restock our dwindling supply of white acrylic paint.

Busted.

Yes, there are moments and days when I still find myself wondering whether we will HAVE enough.

Scarcity sucks.

Maddie's Perspective

This explains so much. Growing up I remember asking my parents about our family's financial situation.

We seemed to have enough money for some things like family vacations but not enough for other fun things I wanted to do.

Now I understand that with my dad's scarcity mentality, it didn't matter how much we had.

He was always afraid of running out.

It's sad, really. Imagine chasing after something but knowing that you'll never get ahead enough to stop chasing.

Questions to Ponder:

1. How does scarcity show up in your thinking (even when there may not be anything lacking)? Could it be disguised as being responsible or frugal?

———

2. What decisions have you made based on fear? This could be a big decision like taking the job that offers more money even if it's not the job you really want. Or it could be an ordinary choice like what to eat and the fear of carbs or calories, etc.

———

3. How does a scarcity mindset limit your generosity? Don't just think money, consider your time. How does scarcity affect your generosity in relationships?

———

4. What would change if you were to adopt a new way of thinking? If you truly believe that there is more than enough to go around: enough money, enough time, enough clients and customers, how would that change your next conversation?

———

FOUR GREEN HOUSES

EARLY-2000S: OAK CLIFF (DALLAS)

W e lost over six figures in the deal. It's the most money I've lost on a single deal.

Past, present, and hopefully future.

The real cost wasn't just measured in the dollars that were no longer in my bank account. There was the lost time, all the stress, the gray hair.

How do you put a price tag on all that?

We invested in an eighteen-unit apartment complex in an inner-city neighborhood of Dallas, not far from the Texas Theatre, the place where Lee Harvey Oswald was arrested after the JFK assassination.

History had passed through there in the 1960s, loudly and publicly. In the early 21st century, it was just a hard neighborhood trying to survive.

For us, this deal was a milestone.

It was a starting point. A proving ground. Something small enough to manage and big enough to matter.

It would be the first of hopefully many commercial real estate investments. In the Monopoly sense, it was the first of four "green houses" needed to trade up to a "red hotel".

Four green houses into one red hotel

I was beyond excited. If things kept going like this, I might be able to "retire" before I turned 30.

I don't mean stop working. The goal was to generate enough passive income from investment properties to cover our bills and enable a comfortable lifestyle.

Just like all the gurus in the books I was reading and seminars I attended were teaching.

And once we overcome the death grip of the rat race, we would be free to spend our time and resources investing in doing more good in the world.

First of many, I thought. I hoped.

A few days after closing, my business partner and I went down to the property to meet the tenants, walk the units, and make some plans.

We were not prepared for what awaited us.

In one apartment in the bathroom, the ceiling above the tub and the wall behind the toilet were both covered in black mold.

The tenants upstairs had tried to fix their broken toilet by themselves. They got a new toilet, put it on top of the flange, and bolted it to the floor.

I'm not sure if they didn't know or didn't care, but they neglected to spend a few bucks to get a wax ring.

So with every flush, dirty water would spill out onto their floor, seep under the baseboards, soaking the drywall, and eventually dripping down into the unit below.

That didn't stop them from using the toilet, though.

I could not believe what I was seeing.

It was early summer in North Texas, which means the weather is hot and moist. Nothing is going to dry out naturally. This problem would not fix itself or go away on its own.

In the following days, we had to move tenants into other units, gut the downstairs unit and even the one next to it.

Once we started opening up walls, we just kept cutting and cutting and cutting. Mold, drywall, insulation. We ripped it out.

All of it. Gutted.

Half of the building was affected.

What I didn't know that day was that it would take us almost three years to get out of that deal and more than a decade to recover financially.

I grossly miscalculated how difficult it is to turn a profit with integrity. I was naive to the complexities and intricacies of being a landlord: delinquent tenants, aggressive vendors, regulations, and most surprisingly, citations.

What started out as optimism and excitement and a lot of hot air about helping people and making a difference, quickly fizzled.

Break even would have been a smashing success, given how much of an education we were getting. That was a nice dream. In reality, we were bleeding thousands of dollars every month, with no end in sight.

As a Boy Scout, we were taught to "leave the campground cleaner than you found it", and presumably that applied to other situations in life as well.

In the end, this was not a campground I was able to clean up. Yes, I didn't make it any worse. But still.

Mediocrity is difficult to celebrate. Please tell me there's not a trophy for status quo.

Maddie's Perspective

Let's put all good intentions and making the world a better place aside for the moment and make this really simple.

If you give with the expectation of getting something in return, that's not giving.

That is a business transaction.

Or a risky investment to be avoided.

Questions to Ponder:

1. Do any of your personal relationships feel more like a business transaction? Do you give and give, hoping to get something in return?

---

2. Have you been in a situation where your generosity is assumed, perhaps without being asked? Boundaries are important. Protecting yourself doesn't make you selfish.

---

3. Think back to any gifts you received this past year. Did any of them feel like there were strings attached?

STORY OF LOVE

WINTER WONDERLAND

JANUARY 1, 2025: GRANBY SKI RESORT

N ew Year's morning, 2025. Ten below zero. I was up early, which usually meant something was wrong.

Climbing into a van before sunrise, I was headed to the ski slopes to try snowboarding for the first time.

I'm not sure how many people decide to take up new sports in their fifties. I had never been skiing before.

Skiing seemed safe. Maybe too safe.

Snowboarding sounded more high adventure. More extreme.

I convinced myself this was a good way to start the year.

New year, new plan, new challenge.

Reset the system. Push the edges a little.

The moving sidewalk carried me toward the top of the bunny slope, humming like a conveyor belt at an airport.

I scanned my lift ticket wrong three different ways (and really frustrated the attendant). I was a total newbie.

Strapping into the snowboard, some guy gave me the only instruction he thought I needed:

"Just keep going. You'll figure it out."

I took a deep breath in, my lungs filling with cold, dry air. Wow, I was really out of breath. And desperate for more.

It was at that point that I wished I had done even a tiny bit of prep or research.

Surely there are a zillion videos online I could have watched so I didn't make a total fool out of myself. Oh well, too late.

I leaned forward, pushed off, and immediately caught an edge.

I launched myself face-first into a very cold, very solid version of snow that felt only slightly softer than concrete.

I sat up, adjusted my goggles, and tried again.

This time I fell on my side.

Then my elbow.

Then my hip.

The next several attempts were a symphony of crash landings. I think I bruised every bony part of my body on the way down.

With each crash, the numbness and frustration increased, while my confidence eroded.

Why can't I be instantly good at every new thing I try?

I could almost hear my mom singing:

Have patience.

Have patience.

Don't be in such a hurry.

Oh, how I despised hearing that song when I was a kid. For whatever reason, that morning it made me smile.

By the time I reached the bottom, I was a collection of fresh bruises and sore bones strapped to a snowboard.

A chorus of conflicting thoughts in my head argued:

Let's go again.
No way, just give up.
Come on, you'll do better next time.
What if I don't. What if I get (more) hurt?
Oh, don't be such a baby. Get your ass back up there.

So back up to the top I went to try again.

And again.

And again and again.

Erik and Maddie in Colorado, January 2025

Halfway down another run, I crash-landed and screwed up my ankle. I wasn't sure if something had snapped, crackled, or popped, but it definitely hurt.

If you've never worn snowboard boots before, they're similar to inline skates, except they're super comfortable. And supportive. And stiff, very stiff.

They basically stabilize and neutralize your ankle from moving. As I was learning that day, as long as you don't take snowboard boots off, it's possible to ignore the pain and keep going.

Truth?

I was tired.

I was stretched thin.

There was so much noise in my head.

Work stuff was anything but simple. A new course I launched a few days earlier had zero signups. My mom's health was declining. Money was tight. The markets were behaving like toddlers on espresso.

I knew I didn't have any extra bandwidth to handle another catastrophe or emergency.

I was "in the red" and there was no backing off.

I had the pedal to the metal.

Full speed ahead.

And that's how it was that day on the mountain.

Keep on going, keep pushing forward, and don't look back.

I did a few more runs (yes, on the bunny slope) and even got adventurous and went on the lift twice.

My favorite part was seeing my daughters and granddaughter ski for the first time. They all took lessons. Smart.

Hazel skiing in Colorado, January 2025

Somehow I made it through the day.

When I finally peeled off the boot that night, I could no longer walk. I tried to stand up, but I couldn't put any weight on my left foot without radiating pain all through my leg.

Had I really gone all day on a broken ankle?

Pretending everything was fine hadn't fixed anything.

The next morning, when everyone returned to the slopes for another day of winter wonderland, I stayed back in the cabin with my foot elevated, surrounded by silence.

It was a new year, but nothing was different.

Not really.

Sure, the view had changed. I live at sea level by the beach, not in a snow-covered mountain village.

But it was still the same old me.

My current operating system wasn't working anymore.

BE → DO → GIVE → HAVE

There didn't seem to be a whole lot of enjoying the HAVE lately.

Why was that? What was I missing?

We had stuff. We did things. We were on a ski vacation, after all. It's not like life sucked. Still, something wasn't right.

Looking out the window, I noticed it had started to snow. I hobbled over to the door and went outside on the porch.

The air was cold and crisp, which reminded me of yesterday morning's adventures on the bunny slope.

Today was the day I was supposed to go down a Blue, and fully expected Maddie would convince me to do a Black.

Nope. Not gonna happen this time.

It was only day two of this new year where nothing was going as planned.

Awesome.

Happy New Year!

Maddie's Perspective

I remember this day a little differently. I knew my dad had been stressed about work and the health of my Gramma.

I tried to give him a pass.

But he had his grumpy pants on that day, and it didn't matter what anyone said or did, nothing helped to shake his mood.

He was right about one thing. His operating system was broken.

This wasn't the first time that his mood had cast a shadow on a family vacation.

Looking back, maybe this was the beginning of breakthrough.

Questions to Ponder:

1. What areas of your life are you so focused on achieving a certain goal that you lose sight of the people and relationships?

---

2. What warning signs are you ignoring? Pain and stress related illness (like headaches and digestive issues) are ways that your body is trying to get your attention. Something needs to change!

---

3. Recall a moment in your life where you knew things were not as they should be. That fork-in-the-road where you could continue down the same path, the easier path, or you could pivot, make a change and try something new. Change is hard, but it's never too late, and it's always worth the effort.

LOVE IMMORTAL

JANUARY 24, 2025: MEDICAL CITY PLANO

The highway was still half-asleep when I pulled onto it, the kind of pale January morning where the sky can't decide whether to wake up or push the snooze button.

My phone sat face-up in the passenger seat.

I was not going to miss another call.

Three missed calls.
Two were from my dad.
One was my mom's phone.

All between three and four in the morning. I hadn't seen any of them until almost six.

I didn't need to listen to the voicemail to know what that meant. I had only been back home for two nights, but it was already time to turn around and head north again.

Stumbling around in the dark, I had thrown a few things into a suitcase, hopped into the car, and finally pressed play.

It was my dad, from the middle of the night.

My mom was in the Emergency Room.
They performed CPR on her.
She's stable (for now).

Reading between the lines, it sounded like my mom made a move to cross over, and modern medicine brought her back.

So there I was, driving north on I-45.

I kept thinking about the last word she said to me:

Jellyfish.

It was only a few days earlier, that Sunday.

My mom was back in the hospital with a nasty infection.

This time when we went to visit, we had to suit up with gowns, gloves, and plastic over everything to keep her safe.

Things had definitely escalated.

And they were not trending in the right direction.

Once I got suited up, I walked over to her bedside. She opened her eyes when she saw me.

I said, "I love you".

Her eyes sparkled.

She said, "I love you" only it came out all slurred and breathy, sounding more like:

Oh-oh Eye-eye-yay You-ou

It didn't matter. I knew what she meant.

We were communicating.

I was catching my mom up with all that had happened in the past few weeks.

This took the form of a rambling story that included sunsets in Key West, a visit to our favorite beach in Mexico, and somewhere in the trip down memory lane, jellyfish came up.

I laughed as I remembered the year there were all those cabbage-heads that washed up onto Galveston beaches. Somewhere in there was the original jellyfish story from Corpus Christi (the one with the meat tenderizer).

My mom wasn't saying anything audible, but her eyes were speaking, letting me know she was remembering, too.

It was a strange conversation with my mom.

Normally she would do the majority of the talking, or at least win the prize for asking the most questions. Her curiosity was insatiable. She wanted to know everything.

This was different.

I was the one doing all the talking.

Her communication was almost entirely non-verbal.

The last time I had seen her a few weeks earlier, it had been complete sentences, full smiles, and questions.

I finally stopped talking.

I just smiled.

And then she said it.

Jellyfish.

I leaned in.

She said it again.

Jellyfish.

"Jellyfish?" I repeated back to her, trying to understand.

She gave a tiny nod, and then for a third time:

Jellyfish.

I nodded, and repeated back to her again, "Jellyfish."

Turning to let the family know she was speaking. I asked when was the last time she had communicated. Maybe earlier that day, or was it yesterday? Time runs together in hospital rooms.

When I turned back around to continue with my mom, the moment had passed. We had a few more eye exchanges. There was a little smile. But no more words.

Jellyfish was the last word I ever heard her say.

Three times (just to make sure I knew how important it was).

That was only five days ago, but it seemed like a lot longer.

So much had happened in such a short amount of time.

That afternoon, I was in the hospital room with my mom.

It was just the two of us.

I opened my computer, pulled up the app that has the answers for everything, and typed in a one-word prompt:

jellyfish

I started reading about characteristics, habitat, and species.

The fourth one on the list caught my attention: *Turritopsis Dohrnii*, a.k.a the immortal jellyfish.

Intriguing name.

I had never heard of this species before.

more about immortal jellyfish

These guys are tiny (less than 1/4" or 5mm wide).

Did you know the immortal jellyfish can revert from its adult form back into an adolescent form when under extreme stress?

It has the ability to return to the start of its life cycle and re-enter its community as a reproducing member.

Translation:

It can go through puberty again.

Go through puberty again? No thanks!

That sounds terrible, if you ask me.

Puberty was not fun the first time around. And I can't say I'd really want to go back and repeat it.

Joking aside, this seemed to defy basic biology.

A rebirth, triggered by crisis.

Reverting to a previous, more life-producing, healthier state.

Fascinating.

Then I saw a picture of the immortal jellyfish.

I clicked on the image and zoomed in.

I saw a vibrant color right in the middle of its otherwise translucent body.

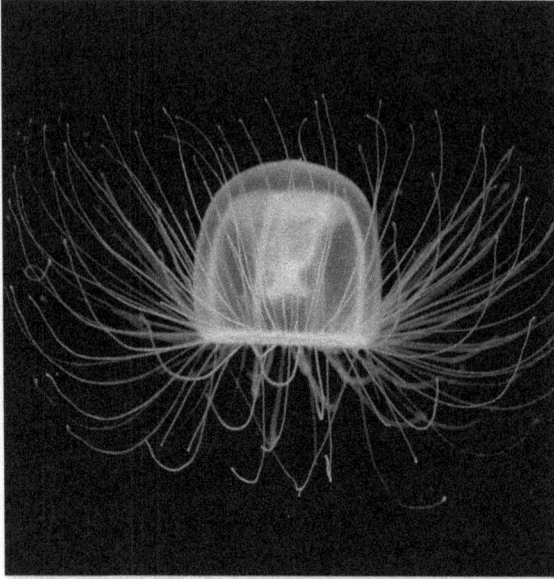

Turritopsis Dohrnii - Immortal Jellyfish

I'm not going to blame it on the dim hospital lighting or my fifty-year-old eyes. That red shape looked like a heart.

And hearts make me think about LOVE.

That's when I knew I had to change the fourth word.

LOVE is always there in the past, the present, and the future.

My mom's love for me began even before I had consciousness. Her love was there from the beginning and each and every day of my life, including today.

Similarly, I've loved my mom for as long as I can remember. I didn't know what tomorrow would hold, or how many more tomorrows there would be.

The timeline was irrelevant. Love cannot be bound by time.

Love would accompany my mom from that hospital room to the next one, and then to infinity and beyond.

A few days later, I would use the Four Words, BE DO GIVE LOVE, at my mom's memorial service. It was my attempt to sum up all she taught me in life. And it was also a nod to brevity, a playful irony because she was one who enjoyed many words.

My love for her continues to this day. Like the immortal jellyfish that can continue living indefinitely, there is no end to love.

Love is immortal.

Mom flying a kite on Galveston Beach, 2000-something

Maddie's Perspective

Everyone has their own way of handling grief and loss.

Maybe one day I will share my story of how I experienced the grief of my Gramma's death, but for now I will focus on my dad.

I have watched him go through all the stages of grief as he was working though the Four Words and the different versions of this book.

It would have been easy to get stuck in the anger stage or the depression stage, but writing has been therapeutic for him and continues to bring him clarity.

When faced with loss, you stop pretending that the things you chase after will last. That's the trap of HAVE.

LOVE doesn't disappear.

It just changes form.

Questions to Ponder:

1. How has loss helped you to slow down and search for clarity?

2. If love is the only thing that endures, regenerates, and gives life (not achievement or possession), how does that truth help you to rearrange your priorities?

3. How do relationships change when you focus on loving someone instead of focusing on what you get out of the relationship?

PROXY HUGS

DECEMBER 2018: BUCERÍAS, MEXICO

There's one more story that belongs in this book. This story is not about my mom or an adventure with Maddie. It is a story about moms and sons and hugs.

I had just finished leading a chair yoga class for seniors, under an outdoor pavilion in Bucerías, Mexico, near Puerto Vallarta.

This was the penultimate stop of a weeklong service trip offering classes at nearby orphanages and rehab centers.

It was a labor of love, and our team was still full of energy, despite the grueling itinerary. When the chair yoga session finished, one of our team members came forward and asked if he could say a few words.

"I've been watching from the back," he spoke into the mic, scanning the room.

Another team member grabbed a second mic and started translating into Spanish.

"I feel that someone here—a mother, maybe—hasn't seen her son in a long time," he continued.

He paused and then took a breath.

I am not your son.

I'm not here to replace him.

I don't know why it's been a long time since you hugged him.

But… if you want a hug today, I'll be right over there.

He pointed to a spot near the corner.

Then he handed me the mic and stepped down.

Seniors chair yoga in Mexico, December 2018

The sound of metal chairs scraping against concrete began to rise to a dull roar.

Nearly all of the seniors, women and men, began to stand up and started shuffling to get in line.

The program director told me he'd never seen anything like this.

I had been coming to Mexico monthly that year, stopping to see this group of seniors each time. They were one of my favorites.

But this was the first triple-digit crowd I had seen.

One by one, they approached my friend.

He took each person's hands and looked them in the eyes. With the help of a translator, they talked. About their son. Their story.

And then came the hug.

Some were quick, some lingered.

Something sacred was unfolding in real time.

I did not have the language of the Four Words at this time. This was back in the BE → DO → HAVE days, in my 40s.

I do remember being simultaneously in awe with what was unfolding in the moment and the impact it was making on everyone present.

And concerned we were going to be late to our next (and final) stop on the trip. There was still an itinerary, an agenda, a plan.

While I hadn't yet made the GIVE connection, it's obvious looking back at this story that my friend's Actions (DO) were coming out of his Identity (BE).

He wasn't giving hugs to get mentioned in a book. He was simply responding to a conviction in his heart and had the courage to act.

A hundred hugs later, you would think he would be drained.

It was the opposite.

We made it to the last stop on time and were greeted by energetic kids ready to twist their bodies into animal poses and make funny noises.

He was right in the middle of the action. This time with seven and eight year olds instead of 70 and 80 year olds.

The same heartbeat echos, no matter the location.

That day, I saw the Four Words lived:

BE → DO → GIVE → LOVE

Maddie's Perspective

I was not with my dad in Mexico for that trip. My sister, Ashlin, was there, and I've also heard her talk about that day. It definitely impacted both of them.

What gets me is that it's so simple. A hug.

Literally anyone can offer a hug.

I'm not saying you should go hug everyone. But in terms of how much it costs, a hug is practically free.

Kind of like laughter. And smiles.

Little things can make a big difference.

Questions to Ponder:

1. Think back to a "random act of kindness" that someone did for you. How did it make you feel?

2. Make a list of people in your life and write down a few simple ways you can show you care.

THE RIPPLE EFFECT

Words matter.

Reflecting on the *year where everything fell apart and had to be put back together*, I am still amazed by how far apart LOVE and HAVE are.

Immeasurable, perhaps.

So much of life is lived chasing the illusion of gaining or having: possessions, titles, recognition, achievements. The list is endless.

It's like we believe in the *pot of gold at the end of the rainbow*. We keep on chasing after it, day after day, year after year. Even when we manage to grab onto a little success, it doesn't take long to recognize that there will always be another pot of gold.

A bigger one. A better one. A fancier one.

As long as we are focused on HAVE, we can never truly be satisfied. HAVE is a vacuum, like a whirlpool or a black hole sucking everything into itself.

HAVE is temporal and fleeting. LOVE is continuity.

The only thing that continues forever is LOVE.

I like to think of the Four Words in terms of the Ripple Effect. We all know the image of a the raindrop hitting a still pond, sending out neat circles. If the whole world lived by *Be Do Give Love*, perhaps those ripples would turn into tides.

Imagine leaders, families, and communities choosing to give rather than take. Every act of generosity would amplify another, multiplying the impact instead of diminishing it.

In business, in relationships, and in daily choices, what if the center of gravity shifted from consumption to contribution? The impacts of that kind of thinking would grow into tides strong enough to change the world.

If we remove HAVE as the end-goal or destination and still preserve the alignment of actions (DO) with identity (BE) and impact (GIVE), we end up with this napkin sketch:

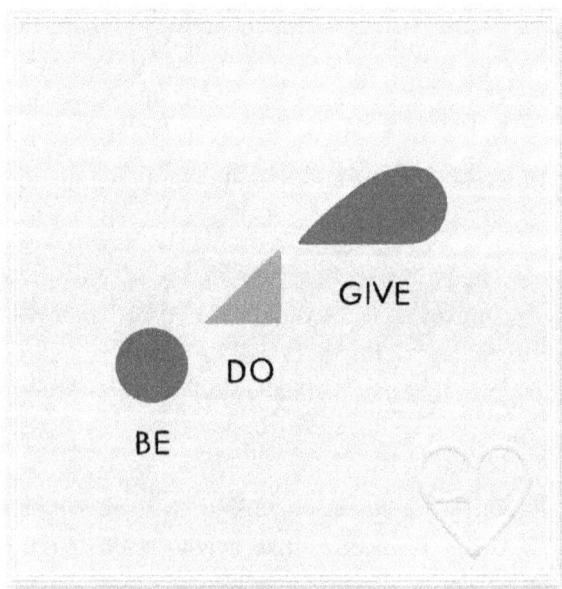

Napkin Sketch BE DO GIVE

So how do we get the fourth word, LOVE, into the drawing?

Great question! It's not by adding another shape.

We already have all the elements.

They just need integration.

By repositioning the elements BE, DO, and GIVE, the fourth word, LOVE, becomes the energetic bond.

BE DO GIVE LOVE

Napkin Sketch BE DO GIVE LOVE

That beating heart of *Be Do Give Love* is the Ripple Effect.

I can't stop thinking about the the Four Words. I'm not sure I want to stop thinking about them.

Maybe in the next book, I'll go into more detail about the how, when, and where. There is more to unpack. For now, I'll leave you with encouragement:

> BE yourself (only you can be you), DO the things that make an impact, which is your GIVE, and most of all LOVE one another.

ABOUT ERIK

Erik Larson

Erik Larson is a Strategic Advisor and Chief Technology Officer (CTO), who transforms teams and technology into highly effective and scalable systems that learn and adapt. His passion comes from a diverse background spanning education, software development, cloud architecture, and private equity tech transformation, where he has participated in hundreds of successful transactions over the last decade.

ABOUT MADDIE

Madailein Larson

Madailein (Maddie) Larson is part of the next generation of storytellers and leaders, and co-author of *Be Do Give Love*. She is currently studying at the University of Arkansas, graduating in 2026. On the stage and on the page, Maddie's voice brings vulnerability, humor, and courage to conversations about resilience, identity, and love.

BOOKING INFO

Erik Larson and Maddie Larson are available for keynotes, workshops, and facilitated sessions where the lessons, stories and framework of *Be Do Give Love* align with your event.

Maddie and Erik in New Orleans, April 2025

Together, they bring a rare intergenerational perspective to conversations about identity, purpose, leadership, work, legacy, and what actually matters when the noise falls away.

For booking, contact books@coroin.com

For more information, visit:
https://coroin.com/books

Speaking formats include:

- Keynote presentations (30–60 minutes)
- Workshops and facilitated discussions
- Conference sessions and panels
- Leadership and generational communication sessions

Example session topics:

- **Bridging the Generational Divide at Work**
  - From misunderstanding to faster alignment, trust, and collaboration across age groups
- **Identity ≠ Performance**
  - Helping people stay engaged, resilient, and effective without burning out
- **Scarcity Is the Enemy of Culture**
  - Replacing fear-driven behavior with trust, generosity, and proactive decision-making
- **From Transactional to Trusted**
  - Building teams that take ownership and stay longer

COROIN BOOKS

In addition to *Be Do Give Love*, Coroin Books has also published the works of Richard W. Turner, Sr. (Erik's grandfather, Maddie's great-grandfather).

Richard W. Turner, Sr. (1924-2004) was a World War II veteran, decorated pilot, artist, author, and devoted husband and father whose life was marked by service, creativity, humility, and a deep faith.

Lt. Dick Turner, US Army Air Corps, 1944

Born in Johnson City, New York, Turner answered the call of duty, serving with distinction in the China-Burma-India (CBI) Theater.

As a pilot, he flew 72 1/2 missions over the treacherous Himalayan supply route known as "The Hump", an experience that shaped his character and perspective for the rest of his life.

After the war, Turner became a leader in the Boy Scouts of America, raised a family, was active in his church, and enjoyed painting, nature, and whittling woodcarvings.

Richard W. Turner, Sr., 2002

He shared 56 years with the love of his life, Caroline, and began writing in later years to reflect on life's most defining moments.

Third Chance [2nd Edition]

Third Chance

An inspiring memoir chronicling a near-death experience and spiritual awakenings. With heartfelt gratitude, he shares the faith, friendships, and miracles that shaped his life and restored his purpose.

This memoir honors the love of his life, Caroline, and the encouragement and support of his family and community.

Revelation ---at last [2nd Edition]

Revelation ---at last

A heartfelt journey through love, loss, and eternal hope. In this intimate work, Turner reflects on the life he shared with his beloved wife Caroline and the emotional and spiritual path he walked since her passing.

Through personal stories and scriptural reflections, he offers comfort and clarity on the promise of eternal life and reunion with those we love in Christ.

Stories from the Hump [3rd Edition]

Stories from The Hump

A vivid and moving collection of war time memories. The stories from Turner's service as a US Army Air Corps C-46 pilot flying over the Himalayas blend danger, humor, and the unseen hand of God.

Turner captures the courage and faith of those brave airmen who flew The Hump in the China-Burma-India Theater of WWII.

From Boo, With Love
[1st Edition]

From Boo, With Love

The previously unpublished stories and poems of Richard W. Turner, Sr., known as "Boo" to family and friends, a decorated WWII pilot, artist and wood carver, outdoorsman, adventurer, scout executive and lifelong storyteller.

Warm, funny, and deeply heartfelt, this collection preserves a legacy of family, faith, gratitude, and the extraordinary moments hidden in an ordinary life.

www.ingramcontent.com/pod-product-compliance
Lightning Source LLC
Chambersburg PA
CBHW022103020426
42335CB00012B/810